Swen Beyer

Supply Chain Performance Measurement & E-Business Supply Chain Management:
Including a Practical Excursus on the Intel Case

Operations Strategy – Supply Chain Management

GRIN - Verlag für akademische Texte

Der GRIN Verlag mit Sitz in München hat sich seit der Gründung im Jahr 1998 auf die Veröffentlichung akademischer Texte spezialisiert.

Die Verlagswebseite www.grin.com ist für Studenten, Hochschullehrer und andere Akademiker die ideale Plattform, ihre Fachtexte, Studienarbeiten, Abschlussarbeiten oder Dissertationen einem breiten Publikum zu präsentieren.

Swen Beyer

Supply Chain Performance Measurement & E-Business Supply Chain Management: Including a Practical Excursus on the Intel Case

Operations Strategy – Supply Chain Management

GRIN Verlag

Bibliografische Information der Deutschen Nationalbibliothek: Die Deutsche Bibliothek
verzeichnet diese Publikation in der Deutschen Nationalbibliografie; detaillierte bibliografische Daten sind im Internet über http://dnb.d-nb.de/ abrufbar.

1. Auflage 2010
Copyright © 2010 GRIN Verlag
http://www.grin.com/
Druck und Bindung: Books on Demand GmbH, Norderstedt Germany
ISBN 978-3-640-65842-8

Operations Strategy – Supply Chain Management

Supply Chain Performance Measurement & E-Business: Including a
Practical Excursus on the Intel Case

Presented by:

Swen Beyer

Submission date: May 20th, 2010

Table of Content

1 Abstract

The environmental surroundings of most companies have changed radically in recent years. Especially the competitive pressure has risen substantially over the past decades, fuelled by an increased globalization of markets and supply chains. In order to continuously satisfy consumer needs in a timely manner, organizations have to focus on performance and efficiency improvement measures. In terms of supply chain management, performance includes the three dimensions efficiency, effectiveness and flexibility which have to be dealt with on an equal basis. One mean to improve supply chain performance is the linkage between various IT applications involved in the whole supply chain. These efforts and trends are treated under the term electronic supply chain management (E-SCM). There are three major critical success factors for the successful operation of an electronic supply chain. These can be clustered into decision motivation (e.g. a shared vision and a strong motivation), implementation process (e.g. the tight integration of inter-organizational information systems and the re-engineering of inter-organizational business processes) and infrastructure conditions (e.g. agreement upon a shared industry standard). There are numerous benefits of an E-SCM implementation such as increased communication speed and decreased cost in terms of communication, inventory and customer service. Furthermore, E-SCM allows mitigating the bullwhip effect by improving the availability of information throughout the entire supply chain. In addition E-SCM allows organizations to implement an entirely pull-based approach. One downside of E-SCM is the need to make a company's entire business processes transparent, also towards supply chain partners who might be engaged with competitors. A further danger of E-SCM is to over-rely on speed rather than on flexibility.

2 Introduction and Research Purpose

The surrounding conditions of most companies have changed radically in recent years. They have become dynamic, unpredictable and turbulent. The competitive pressure has increased enormously, not at last by the internationalization of the markets. Many domestic and foreign companies are fighting with their products for consumers and offer them a growing, almost infinite variety. The goal of satisfying as fast as possible the needs of consumers, led in recent years to a race that resulted in shorter product life cycles and clock speeds. These trends mean that the products and the underlying value chains are more and more driven by consumer wishes.

Today, in times of crises and weak economic growth, companies in addition are especially forced to maintain or increase profit through efficiency. Time, quality and cost are three success factors that can determine the success or failure of companies. The logistics and the supply chain influence these factors in a great way. It has a significant weight in ensuring that customized products can be offered with functionality, quality and in an appropriate time-frame at competitive prices. The alignment of the company with the ambition to reduce inventory and reduce cycle times, connected to servicing customer needs timely has resulted in the development of the concept of supply chain management (SCM). SCM deals with the coordination of in-house order processing and the inter-company supply chain and thus goes beyond the internal business perspective. The success of a company and its competitiveness will depend on the cooperation with the companies that are in the same value chain or from the same network. The consideration of only internal organizational and process structures alone is not enough for companies to stay in the market anymore.

This paper gives a systematic introduction to the fundamental concepts of supply chain and supply chain management. In the first part it presents the principles of supply chain management and its integration into the business processes. The role of E-Businesses in Supply Chain Management and the underlying challenges as well as success factors will be presented in the second part. A case study on the practical example of Intel implementing the E-Supply Chain solution RosettaNet forms the third and final part before finishing in the conclusion.

3 The underlying concept of Supply Chain Management

3.1 Supply Chain Management as a Success Factor

Companies are not operating in isolation but are members of supply chains, which comprise a whole network of suppliers and customers. Today's competition is less between individual companies but more between entire value chains (Corsten und Gabriel 2004, 4). Advances in information and communications systems and the globalization of markets, foster the desire of reducing the depth of added value within a company. The use of outside services and the therefore consequent decline in in-house productions are common developments by national and international companies. Instead of local and internally oriented optimization, it is important to consider the entire value chain in the overall sense of a global optimization. This is making the overall company processes more complex, leading to a higher coordination effort for the necessary cooperation's. At the same time, the requirements increase, especially in terms of timely satisfaction of needs within each value chain. Therefore the need for an effective linkage, through information and communication systems (using state of the art technology), between all supply chain partners is essential. All these requirements can be met by fostering a proactive management of the whole supply chain.

3.2 Definitions and Objectives

Compared to the emergence of many other management approaches SCM was not initiated by academics, but arose from needs in practice. In the 1980s, an American consulting firm used the concept of SCM for the first time. In 1990, the scientific debate about SCM began the first time with Cooper and Ellram as they worked with the differences of traditional concepts of material flow, logistics and related information sets (Stommel 2003, 19f). The definition of the concept of SCM is very problematic. The discussion of many authors regarding the definitional classification of SCM as part of the logistics, logistics management or as a stand-alone concept illustrates the problematic (Stommel 2003, 21). German literature recognizes the supply chain management mainly as an object of logistics. A representative of this view is among others Prof. Dr. Dietger Hahn: "Supply chain management is the planning, management and control of the entire material and service flow, including the related information and money flows within a network of companies and their areas under successive stages of the value chain in the development, production and cooperate recovery of material goods and/or services in partnership to achieve effectiveness and efficiency" (Hahn 2000,

1065). Therefore supply chain management is one the most important measures for logistics planning and execution.

Supply Chain Management has the task to realize advantages in competition for all parties along the value chain. Competitive advantages can be based mainly on cost reduction throughout the supply chain, and improvements to the (end) customer service for example. The aim of managing the supply chain is to achieve a balance between the goals of high customer-service and low inventory-investment which are often seen as a conflict (Kaluza und Blecker 1999, 123). Furthermore, it is important to note that a supply chain not only consists of different member organizations (see Figure 1) but at the same time creates an organizational system itself (Skjott-Larsen, et al. 2007). Especially the increased globalization and new technologies make it possible for companies to benefit from the integration in supply chains instead of following a vertical integration strategy, i.e. owning suppliers or customers. According to the pull-perspective, the supply chain starts with the customer from which all decisions origin (Skjott-Larsen, et al. 2007).

Figure 1: Illustrative and simplified supply chain process/organizational system

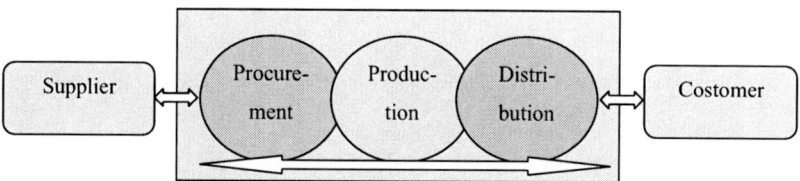

Having defined supply chains, it is relevant to briefly introduce the challenges of supply chains. The integration of several member organizations in one supply chain with their own objectives imposes challenges on managing the supply chain as a whole (Skjott-Larsen, et al. 2007). This is also due to the fact that there is usually no formal organization managing the supply chain (Aulinger 2003, 225).

The ultimate goal of any supply chain must be to manage uncertainty in demand with the existing supply capabilities. (Bayraktar, et al. 2008, p. 194) To achieve that goal, firms have to implement demand forecasting procedures. However, these forecasts are generally not accurate while individual entities along the supply chain increase the inaccuracy with "economical batching decision". (Bayraktar, et al. 2008, p. 195) This information "distortion in customer demand between orders to suppliers and sales to the buyer" (Bayraktar, et al. 2008, p. 193) is termed the *bullwhip effect*.

Performance measurement represents a further management issue in supply chains. According to the definition by the Council of Supply Chain Management, Supply Chain Management (SCM) '*encompasses the planning and management of all activities involved in sourcing and procurement, conversion, and all Logistics Management activities. Importantly, it also includes coordination and collaboration with channel partners, which can be suppliers, intermediaries, third-party service providers, and customers.*' (Skjott-Larsen, et al. 2007, 21). This definition comprises not only the specific activities one typically has in mind but also emphasizes the aspect of coordination. That is especially relevant as members of the supply chain follow their own objectives. Since independent decisions can lead to conflicts, the task of supply chain management is to foster integration. Due to the perspective that a supply chain creates a system itself (Skjott-Larsen, et al. 2007), SCM comprises the management of all decisions for this system.

As one solution to overcome these challenges in supply chain management, the recent approach of electronic supply chain management (E-SCM) will be elaborated on in the following chapters in a theoretical manner. Later, in chapter 7 one E-SCM solution will be explained at the example of Intel.

Performance measurement represents a further management issue in supply chains. According to the definition by the Council of Supply Chain Management, Supply Chain Management (SCM) '*encompasses the planning and management of all activities involved in sourcing and procurement, conversion, and all Logistics Management activities. Importantly, it also includes coordination and collaboration with channel partners, which can be suppliers, intermediaries, third-party service providers, and customers.*' (Skjott-Larsen, et al. 2007, 21). This definition comprises not only the specific activities one typically has in mind but also emphasizes the aspect of coordination. That is especially relevant as members of the supply chain follow their own objectives. Since independent decisions can lead to conflicts, the task of supply chain management is to foster integration. Due to the perspective that a supply chain creates a system itself (Skjott-Larsen, et al. 2007), SCM comprises the management of all decisions for this system.

As one solution to overcome these challenges in supply chain management, the recent approach of electronic supply chain management (E-SCM) will be elaborated on in the following chapters in a theoretical manner. Later, in chapter 7 one E-SCM solution will be explained at the example of Intel.

4 Supply Chain Performance Measurement

4.1 Concept of Performance Measurement

After having defined the concept of SCM, this section will focus on supply chain performance measurement, a particular management issue in supply chains.

Neely, Gregory and Platts (1995) define performance measurement as *'the process of quantifying the efficiency and effectiveness of action'* (p.80). Performance measurement is frequently mentioned as an important management task to achieve objectives (Ackermann, 2003). However, the question that arises is what actually comprises supply chain performance. In 1992 Langley and Holcomb in (Hald 2007) assign supply chain management the role of supporting the creation of customer value. This is in line with the pull-perspective defined above, with all decisions stemming from the final customer. Consequently, (Hald 2007) argues that supply chain performance should assess to what extent the supply chain is currently delivering customer value and also outline how it could be improved. Furthermore, performance in a supply chain includes the three dimensions of efficiency, effectiveness, and flexibility (Hald 2007). Emphasis is put on the importance of measuring supply chain performance, while at the same time pointing to shortcomings of current practice within this field.

While performance measurement refers to the general management task, a performance measurement system is implemented to support this task. This is defined by (Neely, Gregory and Platts 1995, 81) as *'the set of metrics used to quantify both the efficiency and effectiveness of actions.'* One mean to improve supply chain performance is the linkage between the various IT architectures of the different partners involved in a supply chain, as the concept of E-SCM proposes.

4.2 Benefits

A supply chain performance measurement system could help to reduce inefficiencies in the supply chain and increase performance (Holmberg 2000). These inefficiencies often occur since firms pursue their own interests and maximize their own performance (Ackermann 2003). While some authors refer to the alignment of incentives, possibly monetarily aligning goals via a performance measurement system can be seen as another mean. The performance measurement system has the potential to define and measure what is relevant to reach the common goal of supply chain optimization (Narayanan 2004).

4.3 Challenges

Performance measurement systems in supply chains face the same problems as performance measurement systems on organizational levels (Holmberg 2000). A missing link between strategy and measures, a focus on financial measures and having too many isolated measures, include major points of criticism by different authors (Gunasekaran, Patel und McGaughey 2004). A missing customer focus is also mentioned. This is critical in particular in light of the pull-perspective on supply chains as mentioned above, i.e. that the customer represents the beginning of the supply chain.

In addition to these general performance measurement problems, further complications arise in a supply chain context. This is due to the characteristics of supply chains, as spanning across organizational boundaries. One major challenge is the lack of system thinking in measuring supply chains. Due to the characteristics of supply chains it is essential to adopt a cross-organizational perspective (Shepherd und Günter 2006). Since supply chains create an organizational system itself (Skjott-Larsen, et al. 2007) managers should adapt a perspective of the whole entity. Nevertheless, managers tend to focus on activities within their own company (Hald 2007). A main reason for this is that cross-organizational performance measurement involves activities which managers cannot completely control and which are complex. In order to reveal problems in the supply chain, it is reasonable to measure activities which cannot be controlled directly.

Additionally incentive systems on organizational levels might explain why managers tend to focus on the performance of their own organization. These internal incentives system might thereby lead to individuals' behavior that is in conflict with supply chain objectives (Holmberg 2000).

While it is complex to understand how activities in a supply chain are linked, the coordination is extremely important. A lack of understanding of these inter-relations – a lack of perceiving the system as a whole – represents problems for the design of performance measurement systems (Shepherd und Günter 2006).

It is useful to illustrate the problems of incomplete performance measurement systems which fail to comprise the entire supply chain. Integration might span the entire supply chain or only a part. In terms of performance measurement, problems arise if there is a discrepancy between the integration of supply chain flows and what is captured by a performance measure-

ment system. This represents a possible performance measurement system, e.g. on an organizational level or on a department level. The system is only including part of the integrated activities, not measuring complete performance and thus cannot provide useful information to optimize the entire flow.

Even if managers begin to measure *activities* that cross organizational boundaries, the goal frequently remains to measure the individual company's performance and not supply chain performance. Due to the challenges mentioned in this section, companies are currently far from this stage. In order to integrate these inter-organizational activities among the supply chain partners, the greatest challenge remains to harmonize the information flow and foster system integration. A solution to this challenge will be discussed in detail in chapter 6.

4.4 Frameworks

(Hald 2007, 322) defines a supply chain performance measurement framework as a '*method or philosophy designed to measure certain dimensions of supply chain performance*'. This implies that not necessarily one single framework provides a complete picture of supply chain performance.

(Hald 2007) presents a number of frameworks for supply chain performance measurement. Especially supply chain management – involving inter-organizational activities – requires a multi-dimensional perspective on performance (Ackermann 2003). Therefore this chapter will not discuss cost-oriented frameworks but will instead focus on two frameworks; the SCOR-model and the Balanced Scorecard (Hald 2007). While the SCOR-model was developed in a supply chain context, the Balanced Scorecard was originally developed as an intra-organizational management tool.

4.4.1 SCOR-model

The SCOR-model '*is designed as a tool to describe, measure, and evaluate any supply chain configuration*' (Hald 2007, 341). It includes five processes: Plan, Source, Make, Deliver and Return (Hald 2007) and was developed to improve supply performance by measurement (Holmberg 2000). The model provides a standardized categorization for analyzing supply chain performance based on processes and can also be used for benchmarking. Furthermore it introduces a common language, which facilitates communication across the supply chain (Holmberg 2000). Standard metrics for performance measurement along the processes have also been developed. Each process is decomposed into three levels, of elements, tasks and

activities. In terms of performance measurement, on the top level the aggregated performance targets for the supply chain are defined whereas on the third level specific process performance metrics are defined. However, the model's focus on processes lacks the inclusion of customer and supplier relationships. As mentioned above, it provides therefore no complete picture of supply chain performance and (Hald 2007) generally recommends not using any framework in isolation.

4.4.2 The Balanced Scorecard

The Balanced Scorecard (BSC) was developed to overcome short-comings of traditional performance measurement systems, in particular the lack of strategy focus and the exclusive focus on financial measures. Strategy is translated into goals and measures in four perspectives (Kaplan und Atkinson 1998). The original framework includes the following perspectives: *Financial, Customer, Learning and growth*, and *Internal business process*. The ambition is to define and measure multiple objectives linked to strategy and identify the true value drivers. The goal is also to align all objectives and interests across the organization to the strategy (Kaplan und Atkinson 1998). The BSC goes beyond a simple measurement system but rather provides a framework to visualize and communicate strategy. While the combination of balanced measures is one aspect, it is especially the link to strategy that has been emphasized by the developers (Kaplan und Norton, Transforming the Balanced Scorecard from Performance Measurement to Strategic Management 2001). The BSC should visualize the strategy and not just be a collection of measures. Kaplan and Norton (2001) mention that a BSC can also be applied across organizations and also on higher levels involving managers in discussions without anyone being in a dominating position. This is similar to a supply chain situation.

The importance of a balanced performance measurement system has also been recognized in a supply chain context (Shepherd und Günter 2006). The BSC could be applied on a supply chain level, as a strategic performance measurement system and ideally treating the whole supply chain as one organization. An important requirement is that a strategy and shared goals have to be formulated on a supply chain level which can then be translated to the corporate level (Ackermann 2003). A common goal usually shared by all supply chain members includes supply chain optimization and efficiency. According to (Ackermann 2003), an ideal inter-organizational performance measurement system should be balanced, visualize cause and effect relationships and additionally be applied on different organizational levels comprising strategic as well as operative aspects. The BSC with all the characteristics described above therefore seems to represent an appropriate system (Ackermann 2003).

Ackermann assesses how the BSC can be applied on an inter-organizational level after certain adjustments. First of all, he limits the approach to functions within an organization and its key suppliers and customers, rather than the entire supply chain. This is due to practical reasons. It is also mentioned that initially only two firms are involved. A necessary precondition is that the supply chain members perceive the supply chain as one entity. Ackermann argues that this inter-organizational relation should also be formalized somehow despite the fact that supply chains should be able to act flexibly. Only a stable integration allows the application of the BSC.

To be applied on a supply chain level, the BSC needs to be expanded to inter-organizational performance measures and focus even more on non-financial performance dimensions (Ackermann 2003). Additionally, a supplier perspective should be added to the existing four perspectives. Measures within the perspectives also need to be modified and inter-organizational measures should be included. The effects of the supply chain's strategic goals should be measurable on different levels. This means that it should be understandable and visible how different measures contribute to the optimum supply chain performance. This is also emphasized in the recommendations by (Kaplan und Norton, Transforming the Balanced Scorecard from Performance Measurement to Strategic Management 2001). Besides the 'technical' choices of which measures to use, (Ackermann 2003) underlines that the process of finding measures represents the true value. The discussions do not only help to define a common objective and align interests but at the same time foster trust. The importance of trust is also highlighted by (Skjott-Larsen, et al. 2007), as the main driver for collaboration and alignment of individuals' behavior.

Despite the advantages of the BSC, (Ackermann 2003) argues that it might be problematic to implement a hierarchical performance measurement system to a process-oriented supply chain. The SCOR-model (Hald 2007) represents such a process-oriented approach. The argument is further supported by (Skjott-Larsen, et al. 2007) stating that '*the supply chain as a process also requires a process orientation*' (p.364).

5   The relationship between ERP, SCM & E-Commerce

The extremely fast deployment of e-business has astonished many futuristic management thinkers. During our literature research we found out, that only little empirical research has documented the variations of e-business solutions and their key success factors. The current economic turbulences including the credit crunch have slowed down the investment efforts in e-business. Nevertheless many companies are already starting again to reinvigorate their efforts to focus on investments in e-business (Chuang und Shaw 2005).

This chapter presents a conceptual model of the relation between e-business including e-commerce, supply chain management (SCM), and enterprise resource planning (ERP), including a toolbox to determine the significant variables leading to successful implementation of e-business systems.

Unfortunately there exists a significant confusion in the literature concerning the various terminologies used to describe e-business. The core components of e-business consists of: enterprise resource planning (ERP), supply chain management (SCM), and e-commerce (Chuang und Shaw, A Roadmap for E-Business Implementation 2005). The core relationship can be seen in the following Figure 2.

Figure 2: The Relationship between ERP, SCM and E-Commerce

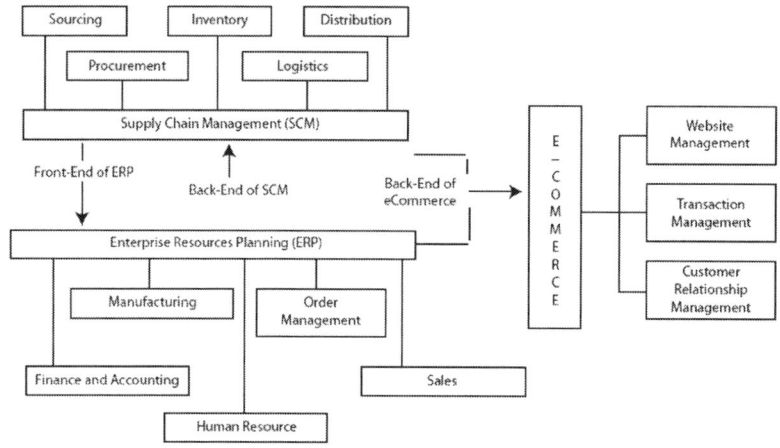

Source: (Chuang and Shaw, A Roadmap for E-Business Implementation 2005, 4)

The first ERP system was found in the manufacturing environment in order to integrate business processes. These systems help companies and their processes to become more flexible

and responsive by creating barriers between functional departments and eliminating duplications. Very often ERP systems are used internally for example in finance, accounting, human resource management, sales and manufacturing. Unfortunately these departments do not have important collaborations with external suppliers and customers. This has changed dramatically with ERP II, which is especially focusing on supply chain management rather than on internal business processes (Chuang und Shaw, A Roadmap for E-Business Implementation 2005, 3).

In contrast the supply chain management (SCM) is considered as a process of interaction with outside suppliers and customers for sharing, exchanging and moving information and goods as already explained in previous chapters. SCM basically consists of actions related to the flow of information and goods which support the transformation of goods from the raw materials stage to the end consumers (Chuang und Shaw, A Roadmap for E-Business Implementation 2005, 4). A challenge hereby is the fact, that the material and information flow goes both up and down the supply chain.

Considering this well supplementary relationship and the ongoing pressure for improvements in the area of time, cost and quality many companies make use of new information technology such as the Internet, and for example offer their products and services on the Web in a so called e-commerce systems. Many companies also use these technological trends to optimize their customer service or operational performance to gain competitive advantage with customer self-service tools, extremely fast response to customer times, shorter product lead times, and optimal inventory levels (Chuang und Shaw, A Roadmap for E-Business Implementation 2005, 4).

After analyzing the major issues in SCM, performance measurements and the relationship with IT systems, the next chapter will now focus especially on the development and trends within the E-business sector and how this is influencing the supply chain.

6 E-Business in Supply Chain Management

6.1 Definition

The following chapter elaborates on the integration of electronic systems in supply chain management. After distinguishing between e-business and e-commerce, the integration of electronic systems into supply chain management is analyzed and critical success factors for inter-organizational information systems, as well as E-SCM benefits and drawbacks are identified.

After the emergence of internet-based business models, terms such as e-business, e-commerce and later m-business and m-commerce have evolved. To date however, these different terms have not been used consistently by scholars in the field. While used synonymously by some, e-business and e-commerce are differentiated by others. This research paper follows the approach of Gerpott (2002) who defines e-business as an umbrella term with e-commerce, m-business and m-commerce as sub-categories thereof. According to this definition e-commerce is the digital initiation, negotiation and carrying out of transactions between different economic entities (Gerpott 2002, 50) while e-business can be defined more broadly as the "execution of business transactions over the internet". (Chopra and Meindl 2001, 391) Gerpott subsequently defines M-Business as a subset of E-Business with the overlap between M-Business and E-Commerce being M-Commerce. In terms of supply chain management the differentiation between e-business and e-commerce is just as important. While e-commerce solely describes the nature of the channel that is used to process transactions with customers, e-business refers to the overall implementation of electronic systems within an organization, including e-commerce, supply chain management (SCM) and enterprise resource planning (ERP). (Chuang and Shaw 2005, 3) The following two sub-chapters will elaborate on the characteristics of integrated electronic systems in supply chain management (E-SCM) and the key success factors of an e-commerce system respectively.

6.2 Electronic Supply Chain Management

The emergence of electronic means of communication and especially the internet have resulted in a substantial impact on supply chain management. Due to an increased price visibility and comparability competition has been fuelled, leaving companies in need for becoming more efficient and respond quicker to market demand. (Lancaster, Yen and Ku 2006, 167) Thus, it is vital for companies to improve communication speed and flow through the entire supply chain. By using the internet as a universally available network, information and feed-

back can be exchanged in or near real-time, enabling an electronic supply chain management (E-SCM) via inter-organizational information systems (IOS). (Lancaster, Yen and Ku 2006, 168) E-SCM extends the general concept of SCM by adding in the use of technology, especially the internet, in order to establish an automated communication network among the different firms in a supply chain. (Lancaster, Yen and Ku 2006, 168) Doing so allows the involved players to reduce paperwork and manual information-keeping such as faxing or telephoning. Further definitions describe E-SCM as "the planning and execution of the front- and back-end operations in a supply chain" (Lancaster, Yen and Ku 2006, p. 168) or the merging of the two fields of SCM and the internet (Akyuz and Rehan 2009, p. 3265).

6.2.1 History

Early measures of improving supply chain management mainly consisted of streamlining internal processes, improving inventory accuracy and implementing standardized record keeping functions. (Lancaster, Yen and Ku 2006, p. 169) With the emergence of computer technology, calculations started to become automated and first MRP systems (Material requirement planning) were introduced. Going along with this change, SCM evolved into a more complex field, now including more and more suppliers and further partners in the supply chain optimization process. Dimensions such as "quality of the materials in use, the on-time delivery of those materials, and customer follow-up" (Lancaster, Yen and Ku 2006, p. 169) became increasingly important while suppliers were no longer seen as sole material providers but rather as partners in an integrated supply chain network. However, at that point the main goal was to improve communication among partners and across firms' borders but not on an integrated end-to-end SCM. An integrated supply chain management was not realized until ERP systems were developed which were able to integrate the large number of previous systems and allowed for intra and inter-firm communication and collaboration. (Lancaster, Yen and Ku 2006, p. 170) For future developments, it is often predicted that supply chains become entirely virtualized with clients pulling products from their initial stages through the entire supply chain. (Lancaster, Yen and Ku 2006, p. 170)

6.2.2 IT in Supply Chain Management

Before the internet became wide-spread, players in a supply chain relied on electronic data interchange (EDI) systems in order to share information. (Lancaster, Yen and Ku 2006, 170) Typically the setup of such an EDI connection required the implementation of a dedicated value-added network (VAN) which provided the network and translation services to run EDI systems. (Lancaster, Yen and Ku 2006, 170) However, due to high costs involved in setting up the VAN-EDI infrastructure, this was a solution that was mainly used by large enterprises

and was not attractive for small and medium-sized enterprises (SMEs). (Lancaster, Yen and Ku 2006, 170) Nowadays, the internet is used to replace the VAN-EDI infrastructure by using virtual private networks (VPN) in combination with extensible markup language (XML) programming. XML is a highly flexible hypertext markup language that allows displaying data in different formats and can be transmitted in real-time via the internet. (Lancaster, Yen and Ku 2006, 170) In comparison to VAN however, using the public internet no longer provides a point-to-point connection which may raise security concerns. However, as VPNs create an encrypted connection and are generally considered as a secure mean for establishing a data connection over the internet, they are the option of choice for implementing information sharing systems in todays' supply chains.

One example for such a solution using VPN and XML is Rosetta Net, a system developed by a consortium around Intel since 1998 with the aim to "create and implement industry-wide, open, e-business process standards." (Sammon and Hanley 2007, 299) RosettaNet is designed to entirely replace EDI solutions and allows suppliers to automate the procurement and accounts payable process while implementing real-time data exchange. (Sammon and Hanley 2007, 299) A more detailed explanation of RosettaNet follows in chapter 7.

6.2.3 The Impact of IT on Supply Chain Integration and Performance

To fully appreciate the impact that the implementation of information systems and IT have on supply chain management, Li et al. propose a conceptual model for the relationship between IT implementation, supply chain integration (SCI) and supply chain performance (SCP). (Li, et al. 2009) In their study, IT implementation refers "specifically to the technical capability to acquire, process, and transmit the information needed for more effective decision making" while SCI is "the ability of a firm to integrate exchange-related activities within functional departments and with supply chain partners." (Li, et al. 2009, 126) SCP finally "includes the dimensions of cost, quality, flexibility and delivery." (Li, et al. 2009, 126) It is important to note that IT implementation and SCI are two distinct dimensions with IT implementation being one measure to improve SCI. SCI in turn depends on human interaction which can be supported by information technology but cannot be replaced by it. In their study on the connection between the three dimensions of IT implementation, SCI and SCP, the authors show that a direct connection between IT implementation and supply chain performance exists but that supply chain integration, which itself is fostered by IT implementation, has a much greater impact on supply chain performance. Thus, they attribute a "bridging function" to SCI, connecting IT implementation and SCP. Examples for investments in IT implementation

that can foster the quality of SCI are systems like EDI, bar coding, enterprise resource planning (ERP), customer relationship management (CRM) and decision support systems (DSS) in accordance with the alignment of IT practices among the different players in a supply chain. (Li, et al. 2009, 132). Due to these findings Li et al. argue that investments that are beneficiary to the extent to which a supply chain is integrated should rather be undertaken than IT investments that seek to improve supply chain performance directly. Improved SCI in turn means improved means of collaboration and integration across the members in a supply chain which will almost automatically result in an improved supply chain performance. Major challenges when implementing IT systems in order to boost SCI is for companies to adapt processes and procedures in order to harness the full potential of such systems. (Li, et al. 2009, 132) Furthermore, the partners in the supply chain have to transform their respective IT systems in order to accommodate for the external integration with their partnering players. Finally Li et al. also acknowledge the fact that although IT implementation allows to improve SCI and SCP, IT implementation is not a source for competitiveness but rather a "competitive necessity" in today's globalized world.

Figure 3: Drivers for Supply Chain Performance

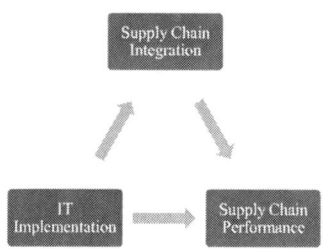

Source: (Li, et al. 2009, 126)

6.2.4   Critical Success Factors for Inter-organizational Information Systems

In their work on the implementation RosettaNet by Cisco and Xiao Tong in China, Lu et al. have identified several critical success factors that need to be fulfilled for a successful implementation of IOS in general. The authors classify these into three different groups: (1) decision motivation, (2) implementation process and (3) infrastructure conditions. (Lu, Huang and Heng 2006, 401) A strong motivation for implementing an IOS is essential since the implementation of such a system is a complex process with numerous obstacles to be overcome. In order to be most effective all partners involved in setting up the IOS need to share this motivation and should at best formulate a joint vision with what their objectives of

the implementation are. (Lu, Huang and Heng 2006, 403) A shared vision on such a project avoids diverging opinions and can in turn lower the risk of the implementation as well as implementation time. The second set of critical success factors elaborates on the implementation process itself. Lu et al. propose a cross-organizational implementation team in order to facilitate the process within the different companies and in order to overcome cultural differences between the involved partners. A further critical success factor is a tight integration of the IOS with internal information systems. (Lu, Huang and Heng 2006, 403) After all, an IOS' success highly depends on the availability of the data to be shared which can only be guaranteed by effective internal information systems (IS). Effective internal IS can greatly enhance IOS goals such as higher data integrity or faster response times while the absence or ineffectiveness of internal IS can compromise an IOS' success. (Lu, Huang and Heng 2006, 402) Furthermore, the implementation of an IOS also requires re-engineering inter-organizational business processes. While some inter-organizational business processes become superfluous (e.g. checking order statuses), others such as information passing can be streamlined due to immediate availability of information among all members in the supply chain. (Lu, Huang and Heng 2006, 404) The third and final set of critical success factors deals with the infrastructure conditions within the internal systems. At first it is vital to an IOS' success to implement mature and reliable internal IS in order to successfully connect them to the IOS. Furthermore, Lu et al. recommend that the involved players agree upon a shared industry standard when implementing an IOS. (Lu, Huang and Heng 2006, 404) There is a wide variety of different solutions that supply chain partners can choose from, ranging from EDI, to Web Based Inter-Exchange (WBI) or XML and internet-based E-SCM solutions such as Rosetta-Net. It should usually be the initiator of an IOS effort to propose a system to be used while the follower partners would typically agree upon the selection. (Lu, Huang and Heng 2006, 404) Conclusively, if all these critical success factors are taken into account during the implementation phase of an IOS, chances for a successful outcome can be greatly enhanced. As previous EDI solutions, internet-based solutions such as RosettaNet also require mature internal information systems, reliable data networks and experienced teams that are willing to co-operate with their respective counterparts from the supply chain partners.

6.3 Benefits

There are several benefits for companies engaging in supply chain collaboration by using E-SCM systems. The most obvious ones are an increased communication speed and decreased costs in terms of communication, inventory and customer service. (Lancaster, Yen and Ku

2006, 170) With E-SCM systems participating companies can share their inventory levels in real time allowing each other to better predict and manage current and needed inventory. As such, E-SCM can also contribute to mitigate the bullwhip effect of distorted demand forecast by improving the availability of information throughout an entire supply chain. (Lancaster, Yen and Ku 2006, 170) Furthermore, due to the high level of integration among the involved players, E-SCM efforts foster long-term relationships between the companies engaging in the respective supply chain network. Opening up their firms towards each other also encourages the development of common strategies and goals which in turn leads to a higher commitment towards the end consumer. Long-term relationships also contribute to stabilized processes since companies can focus on their core-competencies while outsourcing ancillary fields of operation. (Lancaster, Yen and Ku 2006, 171) Apart from that, further benefits are reduced costs. E-SCM systems allow for a supply chain to become entirely pull-based with inventory levels solely depending on end consumer demand. In essence this means, that "a customer places an order which pulls the demand throughout the supply chain." (Lancaster, Yen and Ku 2006, 171) Thus, lower inventory levels can be achieved which in turn lead to reduced costs in warehousing and facilities. A further benefit are reduced data input errors and a generally "more reliable and efficient operations". (Lancaster, Yen and Ku 2006, 171) Finally, E-SCM also affects and improves the customer relationships. E-SCM systems allow anticipating, tracking and responding to customer demand while automatically avoiding stock-outs and rather encouraging customer-driven demand. (Lancaster, Yen and Ku 2006, p. 171) All in all, E-SCM allows corporations in numerous ways to speed up the supply chain processes, to better predict necessary inventory levels and to improve customer satisfaction levels due to faster market response times.

6.4 Drawbacks

Just as there are benefits for companies engaging in E-SCM efforts, there are drawbacks as well. First of all, all players involved in the supply chain need to be dedicated to the E-SCM system in order to make it work efficiently. Data entry needs to be accurate and former methods of information sharing such as faxing or phoning or written records need to be omitted in order to harness the E-SCM's full potential. Another threat for a successful E-SCM implementation is the need for information sharing without restriction which requires a great degree of trust among the involved players. (Lancaster, Yen and Ku 2006, p. 171) Apart from the required trust, benefits of E-SCM solutions may also be unevenly balanced across the different players in the supply chain with large Original Equipment Manufacturers (OEM)

manufacturers benefitting more and smaller suppliers benefitting less. For an OEM E-SCM systems allow for reduced inventory while suppliers need to dispatch more shipments at lower quantities and bear the cost of implementation. Thus, the suppliers' incentive is a less monetary one but rather the hope of locking in an OEM as a strategic future client. (Lancaster, Yen and Ku 2006, p. 172) A further disadvantage of the implementation of E-SCM systems may be the tendency of the involved player to over-rely on speed rather than on flexibility. Especially in cases of distress (such as disruptions in transportation, infrastructure or issues in suppliers' manufacturing) the ability to react flexible in unexpected situations is worth more than speed in the supply chain, particularly since lower safety stock levels will not allow for an undisrupted process otherwise. Further drawbacks for a successful E-SCM system implementation are the necessity to re-think internal processes and link them to the shared E-SCM system as well as the threat of processes to be easily copied. (Lancaster, Yen and Ku 2006, p. 172) Overall, there are several drawbacks to successful E-SCM implementation which mainly relate to integration of internal processes with a shared electronic system, the threat of information sharing and the fear of processes to be copied and the possible over-reliance on speed rather than agility.

7 Case Study: Intel & RosettaNet

7.1 RosettaNet as an example for an E-SCM system

RosettaNet is a consortium of more than 500 information technology (IT), electronic components (EC), semiconductor manufacturing (SM) and solution provider (SP) companies (with Intel being one of the founding members) that strives to create, implement and promote open e-Business services and standards. (Sammon and Hanley 2007, p. 299) Its product RosettaNet – an E-SCM system – enables supply chain partners to exchange information directly, making manual data entries and paperwork obsolete. (Intel 2010) Furthermore, it does not only ensure greater data accuracy but also makes sure that the information in the supply chain is valid and can be processed in real time. (Intel 2010) The overall aim of the RosettaNet initiative is to develop and promote the adoption of universal standards for worldwide supply chain management. (RosettaNet 2010) Applying such best practice principles for E-SCM on a global scale, RosettaNet is set out to: (RosettaNet 2010)

- Reduce cycle times
- Reduce inventory costs
- Improve productivity through automation
- Measure supply chain ROI

To fulfill these objectives, RosettaNet is designed to accommodate the collaboration with various other IT sub-systems that the players involved in a supply chain may use as their back-end ERP systems. (RosettaNet 2010) In order to achieve these objectives, RosettaNet uses the extensible markup language (XML) standard and delivers the necessary communication over the internet. For setting up a RosettaNet infrastructure in the supply chain network of several interrelated entities, the following key standard specifications need to be defined: (Cartwright, et al. 2005, 240)

- RosettaNet Implementation Framework (RNIF)
- RosettaNet Business and Technical Dictionaries
- Partner Interface Processes (PIP)

While the RNIF defines the XML specifications to be used, the Business and Technical Dictionaries establish valid data formats that are to be used across the supply chain. The PIP finally defines sequences of business transactions and responses. (Cartwright, et al. 2005, 240) Examples for such business transaction are purchase orders, web invoices or advanced ship-

ping notifications. Once RosettaNet is set up across the supply chain and integrated with the respective back-end systems, a typical RosettaNet transaction is handled as follows (Cartwright, et al. 2005, 240):

- At first a business request such as a purchase order is generated in a private ERP-system
- The request is translated using RosettaNet Dictionaries and delivered through the RosettaNet infrastructure
- Upon receipt of the request, a confirmation is delivered to the sender
- The request is forwarded into the back-end system of the recipient
- The back-end system of the recipient generates a response and delivers it back to RosettaNet
- The sender receives the response through RosettaNet, unpacks it and can act accordingly

Insulating the different back-end systems from each other, RosettaNet allows the different players to continue using their respective ERP-systems by solely connecting to RosettaNet as a communication interface. While doing so, RosettaNet also provides a secured connection for communication and keeps records of each transaction.

7.2 Implementation of RosettaNet at Intel

Already many years before Intel developed RosettaNet, the company pursued e-business strategies. (Sammon and Hanley 2007, p. 298) Doing so, Intel's "ultimate goal is to become a 100% per cent e-business corporation by marrying internet technologies and critical business systems to increase productivity and competitiveness in the market place." (Sammon and Hanley 2007, p. 298) While in the early 1990's this mission was incorporated by merely using the internet as a corporate communication channel, Intel founded the Internet Marketing and E-Commerce Group (IM&E) in 1995 to consolidate online marketing projects. Later, in 1998 Intel added a global online ordering system and started to promote "paperless purchase orders, shipment notification and deployment processes." (Sammon and Hanley 2007, p. 298) Today, Intel maintains two main systems which allow for the electronic integration of supply chain partners into Intel's supply chain:

- WebSuite (a web-based solution)
- RosettaNet (the above explained system-to-system/business-to-business solution)

After being engaged in the development of RosettaNet itself, Intel eventually fully implemented the solution into its own supply chain, i.e. into its business-to-business automation process and infrastructure in the year 2000. (Cartwright, et al. 2005, p. 239) From the very beginning of the implementation phase, Intel planned to integrate numerous (hundreds to thousands) trading entities (TE) i.e. supply chain partners into their back-end ERP systems. The overall goal of Intel's strive to implement RosettaNet into their supply chain was to increase supply chain speed and enable new business processes that could not be performed without standardized communication patterns. (Cartwright, et al. 2005, p. 244) Rolling out RosettaNet, Intel faced several challenges that resulted from different levels of technology integration and sophistication among their suppliers as well as a wide variety of different ERP systems within their own company. (Cartwright, et al. 2005, p. 241) While large suppliers had already been using EDI systems for communication with Intel, especially small and medium-sized suppliers were not able to easily implement a holistic system like RosettaNet for staffing and investment reasons. That is why Intel developed further interim gateway solutions to complement the RosettaNet standard (Cartwright, et al. 2005, p. 241):

1. Allow existing EDI transactions to continue
2. Create the above mentioned WebSuite for use by less sophisticated trading entities limited to four foundational transactions (Purchase Orders, Forecast, Invoice, Advanced Shipping Notification)
3. Create a File Transfer solution for non-RosettaNet and non-EDI business transactions.

In order to account for the numerous ERP systems that Intel was using and the four different communication gateways (including RosettaNet as the major solution) that Intel offered to its suppliers, it was consciously decided to decouple Intel's backend systems from these public gateways by implementing a Middleware Services Platform (MwS). (Cartwright, et al. 2005, 241) The advantage of a MwS is that it allows to translate data from multiple ERP systems into the respective gateway standards (e.g. RosettaNet). Thus, Intel's backend systems can evolve without requiring changes to the communication infrastructure. Also, connecting the four mentioned gateways (RosettaNet, EDI, File Transfer, WebSuite) to the MwS, TEs are able to switch from one system to another solely requiring Intel to activate another interface for them. (Cartwright, et al. 2005, 242) Figure 4 illustrates how Intel's different ERP systems are connected via the MwS platform to the public gateways which serve as the interface to the suppliers.

Figure 4: Intel Implementation of RosettaNet

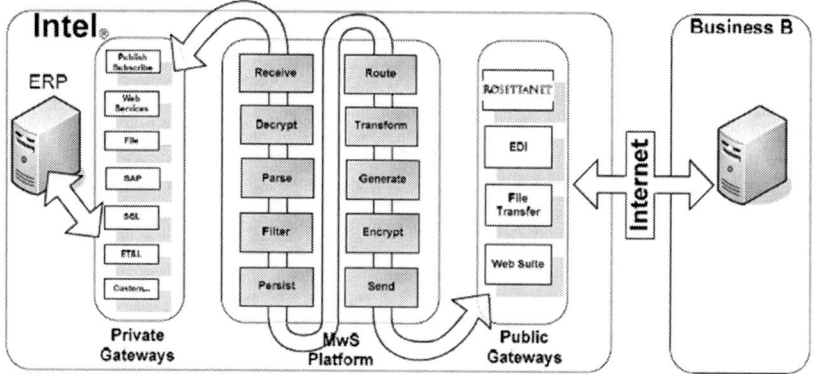

Source: (Cartwright, et al. 2005, 242)

Furthermore, Intel has partnered with so-called "hub-providers" in order to set up a second piece of middleware (or hubs) which converts the data streams of TEs running EDI and File Transfer into RosettaNet compliant standards. Thus, Intel could eventually discontinue the EDI and File Transfer interfaces without requiring every TE to shift to RosettaNet immediately. (Sammon and Hanley 2007, p. 298) This was pursued under the RosettaNet Automated Enablement (RAE) program which is set out to tackle the following downsides that SMEs may encounter when trying to integrate RosettaNet into their infrastructure:

- High cost to develop RosettaNet infrastructure
- Limited expertise to integrate RosettaNet into internal processes
- Time necessary to implement RosettaNet does not justify implementation

From a technical point of view the RAE program enhances RosettaNet by offering TE's the opportunity to display RosettaNet data "in the absence of integration with an implementation". (Cartwright, et al. 2005, 243) Furthermore, it allows TE's to manually feed data into the gateway interface, again without the need for ultimate integration into the own backend systems. This functionality is realized by using the standard presentation metadata PDF/XPF. As an open standard, PDF/XPF allows SME's to use numerous tools in order to respond to and display messages from Intel or other supply chain partners. Integrating this functionality into the gateway interfaces, the only two interfaces left that suppliers use for communication with Intel today are WebSuite and RosettaNet. (Sammon and Hanley 2007, 299)

With the implementation of RosettaNet and the RAE program to further facilitate RosettaNet's usage, Intel has incurred tremendous savings in terms of application development and

re-use, shared infrastructures as well as support and maintenance. Furthermore, RosettaNet enables touch-less transactions, makes manual and error-prone data entry obsolete and allows for automating the "sending and receiving of real-time, up-to-date data." (Sammon and Hanley 2007, p. 299) Apart from these improvements, E-SCM systems have proven to feature the following advantages and cost savings for Intel (Sammon and Hanley 2007, p. 301):

- Productivity improvements (less call volume resulting in improved efficiency, reduced paperwork, less time spent on payment issues)
- Head count reduction
- Increased on-time payments for suppliers resulting in early payment discounts for Intel
- Improved data integrity reducing purchase order/invoice mismatches
- Time savings for personnel allowing them to work on more value-added tasks
- End-users are able to enjoy speed and uniformity in purchasing practices

Overall, the RosettaNet's implementation led to time and money savings for Intel and its suppliers and is an important step for the company in order to achieve its goal of becoming a 100% e-corporation. This view is supported by Intel's E-Business Manager of Ireland who stated "that the main advantage of using RosettaNet is that it gives [Intel] a platform for the future [which] goes a step further on the integration than WebSuite did" (Sammon and Hanley 2007, 301) with WebSuite being the above mentioned and still-in-place predecessor of and alternative to RosettaNet. However, it remains uncertain at which time Intel will actually be able to call itself a 100% e-corporation as this depends on the definition of the term itself as well as the future implementation speed of RosettaNet. The statement of an E-Systems Analyst at Intel Ireland and the WebSuite Development Manager at Intel US serve as a comprehensive conclusion: "I don't believe we are going to get there [to the 100% e-corporation] with WebSuite alone, it will have to be through Rosetta Net" (E-Systems Analyst) and "If you look at [a 100% e-corporation] saying we want all our transactions electronic, realistically I think we are 20 years away from that. [...] If it is not, and some people use it in Intel that '100% e-corporation' means that all our standard transactions are electronic, I think we are probably closer, we are maybe 5 years away." (WebSuite Development Manager). (Sammon and Hanley 2007, p. 302)

8 Conclusion

After analyzing the general concept of supply chain management and identifying levers for performance improvement, the underlying field of research is strongly challenged by a continuous optimization pressure. Driving factors are a strong increase in complexity and permanently growing requirements in terms of time, cost, and scope. Key success factors between all supply chain partners are definitely an effective linkage within the information and also between the communication systems. In order to achieve that goal, firms have to change their management information system and make use of state of the art IT infrastructure. The introduction in E-supply chain management including the impact on performance and benefits, describes theoretically how companies can gain competitive advantages and outperform their competitors. The provided INTEL case presents the successful implementation of the E-supply chain management system "RosettaNet" and how they successfully integrate all supply chain partners into a collaborative planning cycle. This technology combines all supply chain partners in one transparent system where everybody manages critical business activities in order to improve efficiency and effectiveness. It shows in a pragmatic way the need and advantages of an online and real time support for managerial decision making to handle all business intelligence tasks. The underlying research shows clearly, that it is far more challenging to form an e-supply chain using a web based strategic management system than just implementing an ordinary ERP system. In today's web 2.0 or digital economy, successfully companies will be those who can handle the technological and organizational challenges and heading towards web-based integrations. The lack of standardized infrastructures, tools and applicable frameworks appear to be the greatest obstacle for organizations in the near future. Many industries are still searching for a common platform and IT standard in order to provide seamless integrations among all supply chain partners. This fascinating topic still offers substantial room for interesting future research in the areas of standardization efforts and development framework.

9 Bibliography

Ackermann, I. "Using the Balanced Scorecard for Supply Chain Management – Prerequisites, Integration Issues, and Performance Measures." In *Strategy and Organization in Supply Chains*, by S. Seuring, M. Müller, M. Goldbach and U. Schneidewind. Heidelberg, 2003.

Akyuz, Goknur Arzu, and Mohammad Rehan. "Requirements for forming an 'e-supply chain'." *International Journal of Production Research* 47, no. 12 (2009): 3265-3287.

Aulinger, A. *Supply Chains as Strategic Alliances - A Rout Map for Cooperation Management.* Heidelberg: in: Stefan Seuring, Maria Goldbach, Martin Müller, Uwe Schneidewind (Hrsg.): Strategy and Organization in Supply Chains, 2003.

Cartwright, John, Jay Hahn-Steichen, Jackson He, and Thurman Miller. "RosettaNet for Intel's Trading Entity Automation." *Intel Technology Journal* 9, no. 3 (2005): 239-246.

Chopra, Sunil, and Peter Meindl. *Supply Chain Management.* Upper Saddle River, NJ: Prentice-Hall, Inc., 2001.

Chuang, Ming-Ling, and Wade H. Shaw. "A Roadmap for E-Business Implementation." *Engineering Management Journal* 17, no. 2 (2005): 3-13.

—. "A Roadmap for E-Business Implementation." *Engineering Management Journal*, 5 2005, 17 ed.: 1-13.

Corsten, Daniel, and Christoph, Gabriel. *Supply Chain Management erfolgreich umsetzen.* Berlin: Springer, 2004.

Gerpott, T. J. *Wettbewerbsstrategische Positionierung von Mobilfunknetzbetreibern.* Wiesbaden: Gabler, 2002.

Gunasekaran, A., C. Patel, and R. McGaughey. "A framework for supply chain performance measurement." *International Journal of Production Economics*, 2004: 333 – 347.

Hahn, Dietger. *Problemfelder des Supply Chain Management (from: Supply Chain Management).* München: Gabler , 2000.

Hald, K.S. "Performance Measurement and Management in the Supply Chain." In *Managing the Global Supply Chain*, by T. Skjott-Larsen, P.B. Schary, J.H. Mikkola and H. Kotzab. Copenhagen, 2007.

Holmberg, S. "A systems perspective on supply chain measurements." *International Journal of Physical Distribution & Logistics Management*, 10 2000, 30 ed.: 847-868.

Intel. "B2Bi Tools." *RosettaNet*. 2010. https://supplier.intel.com/static/B2Bi/RosettaNet.htm (accessed May 2, 2010).

Kaluza, Bernd, and Thorsten Blecker. *Supply Chain Management und Unternehmung ohne Grenzen, zur Verknüpfung zweier interorganisationaler Konzepte.* Klagenfurt: Wildemann, Horst (publisher), 1999.

Kaplan, R., and A. Atkinson. *Advanced Management Accounting.* 3rd. New Jersey, 1998.

Kaplan, R., and D. Norton. *Transforming the Balanced Scorecard from Performance Measurement to Strategic Management.* Vol. 15, in *Accounting Horizons*, by R. Kaplan and D. Norton, 87 – 104. 2001.

Lancaster, Sean, David C. Yen, and Cheng-Yuan Ku. "E-supply chain management: an evaluation of current web initiatives." *Information Management & Computer Security* 14, no. 2 (2006): 167-184.

Li, Gang, Hongjiao Yang, Linyan Sun, and Amrik S. Sohal. "The impact of IT implementation on supply chain integration and performance." *International Journal of Production Economics* 120 (2009): 125-138.

Lu, Xiang-Hu, Li-Hua Huang, and Michael S.H. Heng. "Critical Success Factors of inter-organizational information system - A case study of Cisco and Xiao Tong in China." *Information & Management* 43 (2006): 395-408.

Narayanan, V.G. and Raman, A. "Aligning Incentives in Supply Chains." *Harvard Business Review*, 11 2004: 94-102.

Neely, A., M. Gregory, and K. Platts. "Performance measurement system design – a literature review and research agenda." *International Journal of Operations & Production management*, 12 1995: 80-116.

RosettaNet. "Rosetta Net - What We Do." *Rosetta Net.* 2010. http://www.rosettanet.org/dnn_rose/AboutRosettaNet/WhatWeDo/tabid/278/Default.a spx (accessed April 30, 2010).

Sammon, David, and Paul Hanley. "Becoming a 100 per cent e-corporation: benefits of pursuing an e-supply chain strategy." *Supply Chain Management: An international Journal,* 2007: 297-303.

Shepherd, C., and H. Günter. "Measuring supply chain performance: current research and future directions." *International Journal of Productivity and Performance Management,* 2006: 242 – 258.

Simchi-Levi, David, Philipp Kaminsky, and Edith Simchi-Levi. *Designing & Managing the Supply Chain.* New York, USA: McGraw-Hill, 2003.

Skjott-Larsen, T., P.B. Schary, J.H. Mikkola, and H. Kotzab. *Managing the Global Supply Chain.* Copenhagen: Copenhagen Business School Press, 2007.

Stommel, Herbert. *Inbound Supply Chain Management in der Automobilindustrie. Ein Konzept zur Steuerung von kundengetriebenen und variantenreichen Zulieferketten.* Berlin: TU Berlin/ Dissertation, 2003.

'

Lightning Source UK Ltd.
Milton Keynes UK
UKOW04f1808281013

219956UK00001B/71/P